This book belongs to:

_____

_____

Brimming with creative inspiration, how-to
projects, and useful information to enrich your
everyday life, quarto.com is a favorite destination
for those pursuing their interests and passions.

Inspiring | Educating | Creating | Entertaining

© 2011 Quarto Publishing Group USA Inc.
Artwork on pages 40–41 © 2004 Peter Mueller.
Photos on pages 6–7 © 2006, 1995 Quarto Inc.

First published in 2011 by Walter Foster Jr., an imprint of The Quarto Group.
100 Cummings Center, Suite 265D, Beverly, MA 01915, USA.
T (978) 282-9590 **F** (978) 283-2742 **www.quarto.com** • **www.walterfoster.com**

Walter Foster Jr. titles are also available at discount for retail, wholesale, promotional,
and bulk purchase. For details, contact the Special Sales Manager by email at
specialsales@quarto.com or by mail at The Quarto Group, Attn: Special Sales
Manager, 100 Cummings Center, Suite 265D, Beverly, MA 01915, USA.

ISBN: 978-1-60058-224-0

Printed in China
10 9

I ♥ Cats!

Activity Book

Meow-velous stickers, trivia,
step-by-step drawing projects,
and more for the cat lover in you!

Table of Contents

Cat Breeds

The Cat Fanciers' Association recognizes 41 different cat breeds. Each breed has its own unique features. Can you see what they are?

Cat Breeds

Abyssinian

American Shorthair

Bombay

Chartreux

British Shorthair

Burmese

Bengal

Exotic Shorthair

Cornish Rex

Devon Rex

Egyptian Mau

European Shorthair

Japanese Bobtail

Javanese

Korat

Havana Brown

Manx

Norwegian Forest Cat

Ocicat

Oriental

Persian

Siamese

Scottish Fold

Somali

7

Singapura

British Shorthair

Siberian

Ragdoll

American Curl

Ragamuffin

Russian Blue

Sphynx

Turkish Van

Birman

Maine Coon

Selkirk Rex

La Perm

8

Drawing Projects

Learn how to draw 16 different breeds of cats by starting with basic shapes and then following step by simple step. Practice your drawings on scrap paper. Once you've mastered each breed, you can add a finished colored drawing to the Sketch Pad beginning on page 79.

Getting Started

When you look closely at the drawings in this book, you'll notice that they're made up of basic shapes, such as circles, triangles, and rectangles. To draw all your favorite felines, just start with simple shapes as you see here. It's easy and fun!

Circles are used to draw a standing cat's chest and hips.

 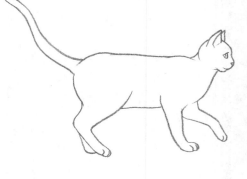

Ovals are good for starting out a seated feline.

Triangles are purr-fect for most cats' ears.

Coloring Tips

There's more than one way to bring your fave felines to life on paper—you can use crayons, markers, or colored pencils. Just be sure you have plenty of good natural colors, such as black, brown, orange, pink, and green.

Pencil

Colored pencil

Crayon

Marker

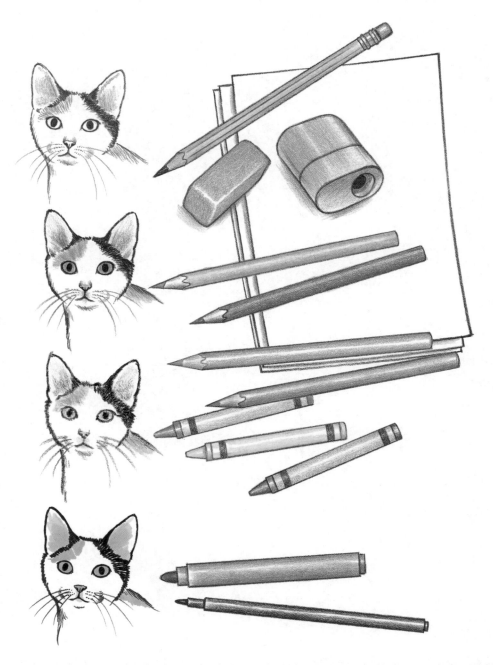

Selkirk Rex Kitten

Selkirk Rex kittens often have shaggy, rumpled-looking fur. When they reach adulthood, their wavy locks become curly coats.

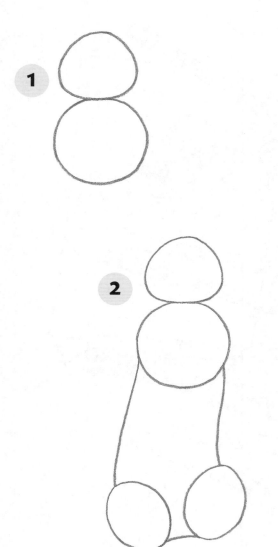

5

6

7

Fun Fact

The Selkirk Rex is a natural breed that was discovered in the United States in 1987. Like the Cornish Rex and the Devon Rex, this breed has a curly coat. But with its stronger, rounder body, it looks very different from its fellow "Rex" cats!

Abyssinian Kitten

Abys are short-haired cats with strong bodies—
and stronger personalities! These curious kitties
are intelligent and outgoing.

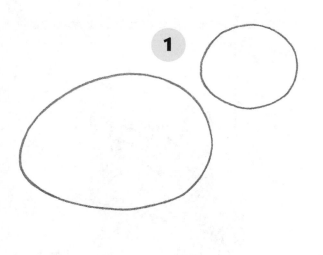

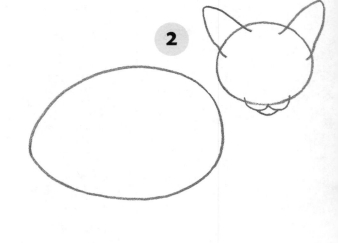

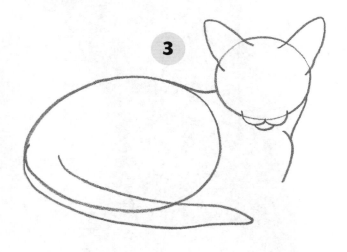

Fun Fact

The first documented Aby came from Ethiopia in 1868—but many believe that this elegant breed is a descendant of the cats of ancient Egypt! The mummified cats found in Pharaohs' tombs are similar to today's Abyssinian in many ways.

Persian

The popular Persian is known for its long, luxurious coat. But its face, neck, body, and legs are all short—as is its bushy tail!

1

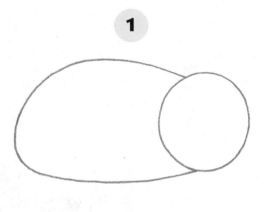

2

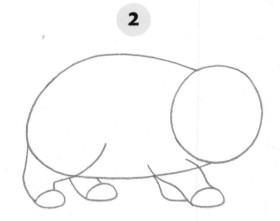

3

4

5

6

Egyptian Mau

The Mau sports both spots and stripes!
And this social kitty has a reputation for
being playful as well as graceful.

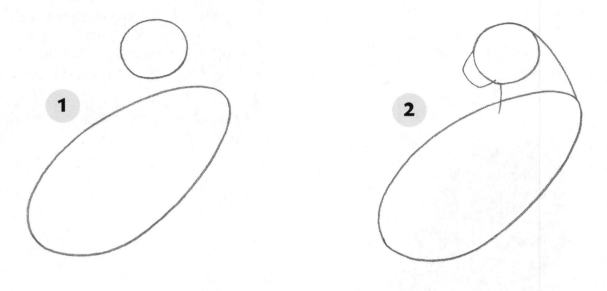

British Shorthair

The best words to describe this feline are large and round! And circles and ovals are the purr-fect shapes for drawing this quiet cat!

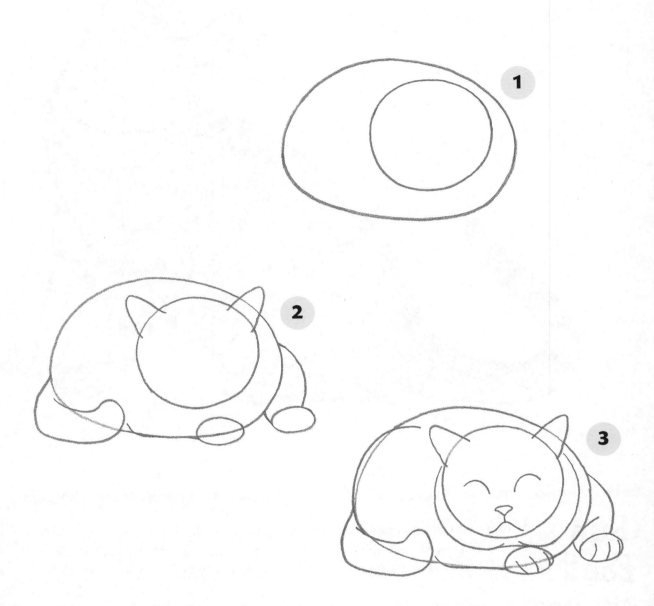

Maine Coon

It's easy to see where the gentle giant of the cat world got its name! This Maine native has a bushy, ringed tail—like a raccoon's!

Fun Fact

The Maine Coon is the oldest American breed and the first native American show cat! Although it now places second in breed popularity, the Coon comes first in size. Some males weigh 20 pounds or more, and this Yankee cat is four times the size of the Singapura, the smallest cat breed.

Ragdoll

This soft, fluffy cat is so mellow that it often flops like a rag doll when picked up! An affectionate breed, Ragdolls love to cuddle.

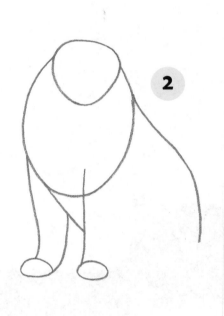

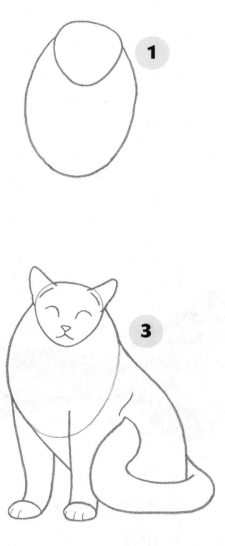

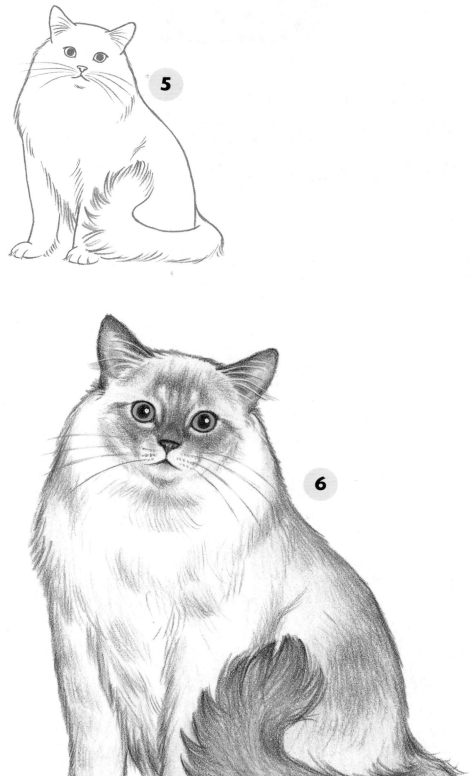

Manx

The Manx is a mouser with only a small bump for a tail! And with its longer rear legs, this kitty shows off its "rumpy riser."

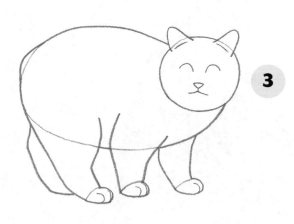

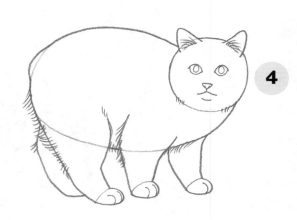

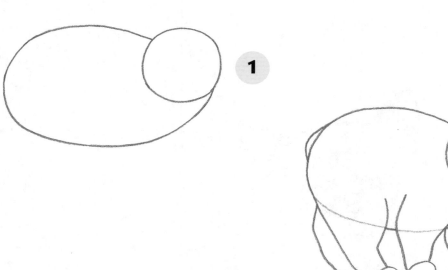

5

6

Fun Fact

The Manx breed comes from the Isle of Man, off the coast of Britain. There tailless cats are so common that when a native farmer learned that rumors about cats having tails were true, he said, "That must look really funny, all those cats with tails."

Turkish Angora

The Turkish Angora is a playful and devoted cat. It's not uncommon for this beautiful, slender breed to have mismatched eyes!

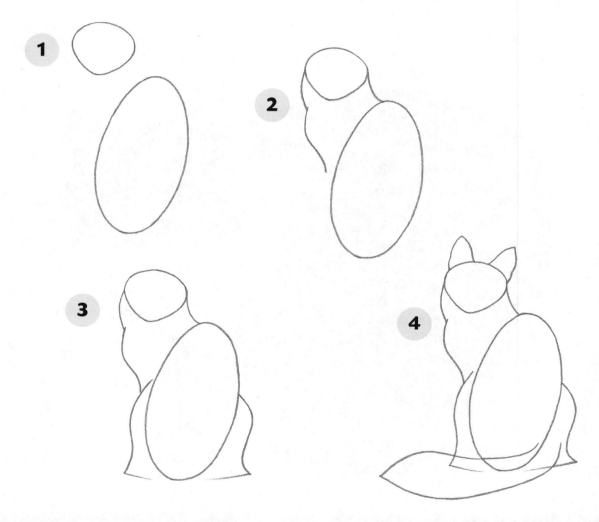

Fun Fact

The Turkish Angora is one of the national treasures of its homeland, Turkey. It was the first long-haired cat to be brought to Europe; in the 1700s, it was the darling of European aristocracy. But the breed lost popularity, and these cats would be extinct today if not for the Turkish zoos that saved them!

Russian Blue

Quiet-loving Blues can happily sit still for hours. To draw this cat in its comfy pose, begin with marshmallow shapes for its head and body.

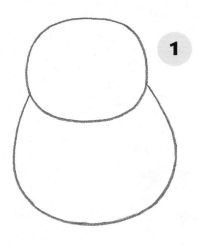

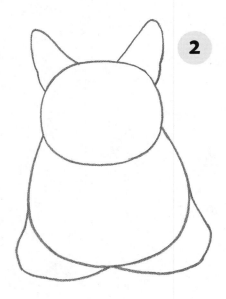

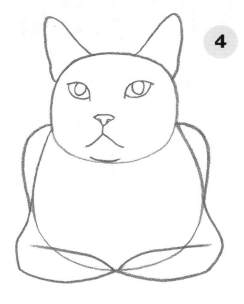

4

5

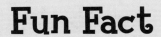

Fun Fact

As you might guess from its name, the Russian Blue comes from Russia, where it was discovered by the British about 200 years ago. This breed has had many names in the past, including "Russian Shorthair," "Maltese Blue," "Archangel Blue," and "Foreign Blue."

Norwegian Forest

This Norwegian is a furry feline with a thick, heavy coat. Its mane and tail are fluffy, and its triangular ears are straight and tall!

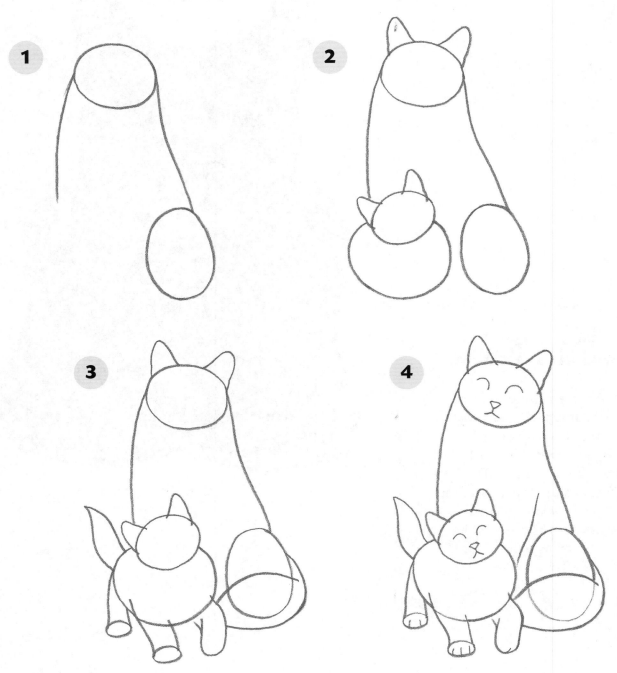

5

Fun Fact

Vikings (Scandinavian seafarers) liked to have cats on their ships to fight pest populations, so they picked up mousers at ports around the world; they brought the first cats to Norway around the year 1000. Cold Nordic winters favored cats with sturdy builds and thick coats, so these imported cats eventually developed into a new breed: Norwegian Forest Cats.

7

6

Scottish Fold

With unusual flat, folded ears; a round head; and big, golden eyes, the Scottish Fold looks like the feline version of an owl!

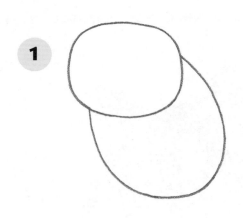

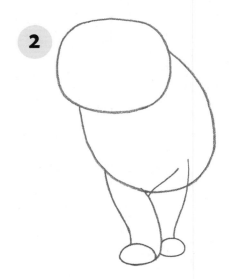

5

6

Fun Fact Scottish Folds aren't bred with other Folds because their kittens can have crippling skeletal problems. To keep this breed healthy, Folds are mated with Scottish Straights (cats from the same bloodline but without folded ears) and American or British Shorthairs.

Ocicat

Despite its large, muscular body, the spotted Ocicat is graceful. This exotic-looking tabby has a long tail that tapers to a point.

Fun Fact

The Ocicat has markings similar to the ocelot, a South American wild cat. But its markings take time to develop. Ocicat kittens have solid stripes along their backs; these lines of dark color separate into spots as the cats age!

Korat

In Thailand, this shiny-coated cat is considered a symbol of good luck! The breed is also known for being vocal and affectionate.

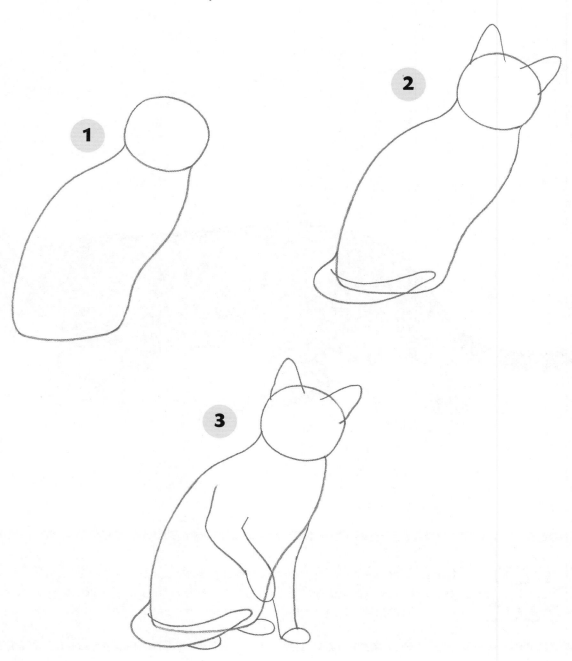

Birman

The round white paws on this breed—also known as "The Sacred Cat of Burma"—distinguish it from other color-point varieties.

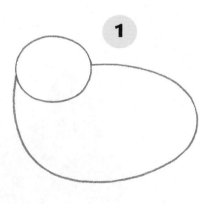

American Curl

The Curl is the only breed to feature ears that curl backward. It's a good thing this friendly feline loves to be the center of attention!

Cat Crafts

What better way to show your kitty you care than to make it a shiny disco ball toy or a personalized food tin? And as a special human treat—have an adult help you bake some delicious cat-shaped cookies!

Retro Kitty Disco Ball

Get your pet's groove on with this glitzy disco ball.

Materials

- 18" wire
- Styrofoam ball
- Masking or duct tape
- 3 sheets black tissue paper
- Scissors
- Sparkle decoupage
- Paintbrush
- Silver wrapping paper

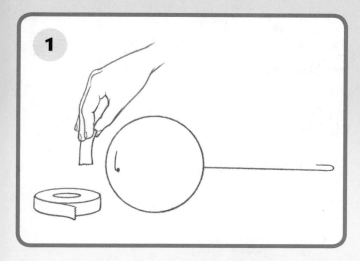

1

◄ First, find an adult to help you with this project. Then poke the wire through the Styrofoam ball, threading it through so that it comes out the opposite end and leaves approximately a 2" "tail." Secure the tail flush with the ball using masking or duct tape. You should have a length of wire sticking out of one side of the ball that will be used as a hanger.

► Cut the black tissue paper into several 1"x 4" strips. You'll need enough to cover the entire surface of your ball twice. Working in sections, cover the ball with sparkle decoupage. Spread and slightly overlap the black tissue paper so that the entire surface is smooth, and coat it with a layer of decoupage as you work around the ball. Allow the tissue paper to dry overnight, and then repeat the process so that you have two layers of tissue. Your disco ball should look solid black and fairly smooth and even. Allow it to dry overnight again.

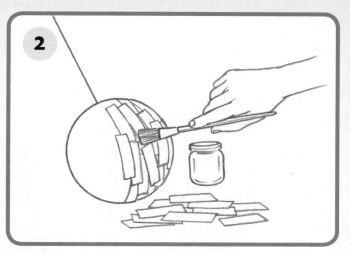

2

◄ Cut the silver wrapping paper into many 1" squares. Set the ball on a small bowl with the wire hanger pointing up. Use decoupage and a brush to paste the silver squares around the center of the ball, leaving small uniform-sized spaces in between.

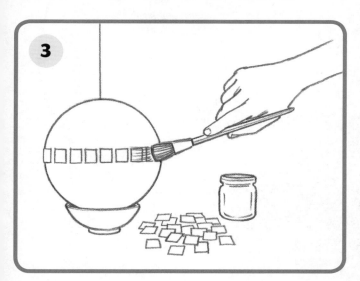

3

► Continue to add squares, arranging them with consistent spaces, like bricks. You may need to trim your squares to fit as you work your way up and down the ball. Continue until the entire surface of the ball is covered with silver squares. Finish with a final coat of decoupage and let the disco ball dry overnight.

4

Kitty Treat Tin

Create a feeding-time frenzy
by designing your own charming chow cans.

Materials

- 2 enlarged color copies of photos sized to cover your paint can
- Clean and empty paint can
- Scissors
- Paintbrush
- Decoupage
- Colorful cardstock
- Craft glue
- Small pet toy or ornament

1

First, find an adult to help you with this projesct. Then, make large photocopies of your photos and line them up around the paint can, cutting holes to allow for the handle. Working one side at a time, use a paintbrush to cover one side of the can with decoupage, and then lay a photo on top, pressing it smooth to prevent bubbles. Make sure to secure the edges.

2

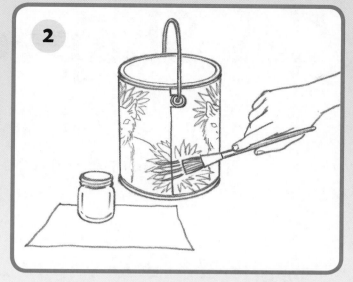

Affix the second photo to the opposite side of the can, overlapping the first layer slightly to ensure a good seal. Allow the photos to dry, and then spread a thin layer of decoupage over the entire surface of the can, covering the photos completely. Allow them to dry for at least 30 minutes, and then apply a second coat of decoupage.

3

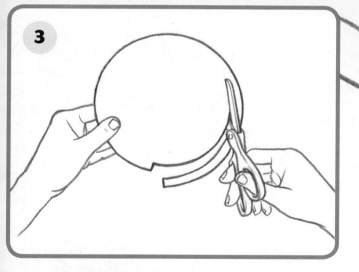

▲ Trace the can lid onto colorful cardstock, cut out the shape, and then trim it to fit into the recessed surface on top of the lid. Attach it to the lid using decoupage.

▶ Use a generous amount of craft glue to securely attach your pet toy or ornament to the center of the lid. When everything is completely dry, fill the can with your cat's favorite treats.

Cat-Shaped Cookies

Grab a grown-up and a glass of milk— these shortbread cookies are delicious!

Shortbread Cookies

INGREDIENTS
2 cups all-purpose flour
¼ teaspoon salt
1 cup unsalted butter, room temperature
½ cup super fine sugar
1 teaspoon pure vanilla extract
Cat-shaped cookie cutter (or a table knife)
Frosting
Candies, chocolate chips, or any other edible cookie toppings

DIRECTIONS
1. Find an adult to help you with, and supervise, this project.
2. Whisk the flour and salt together in a bowl. Set aside.
3. In a large bowl, beat the butter with an electric mixer until smooth.
4. Add the sugar and vanilla extract to the butter and beat for about 2 minutes, until smooth.
5. Gently stir in the flour mixture, but be carful not to overmix.
6. Flatten the dough into a disk shape, wrap in plastic wrap, and chill in the refrigerator for at least an hour.
7. Preheat the oven to 350 degrees.
8. Line two baking sheets with parchment paper.
9. On a lightly floured surface roll out the dough to ¼ inch thick. Cut into cat shapes with a lightly floured knife, or use a cat-shaped cookie cutter. If using a knife, be sure to have an adult help you cut the dough.
10. Place the cookies on the prepared baking sheet and place in the refrigerator for about 15 minutes. This will harden the dough so the cookies will keep their shape in the oven.
11. Bake for 8 to 10 minutes, or until the cookies are golden brown.
11. Once the cookies have cooled, you can use frosting, candies, chocolate chips, sprinkles or any other edible decorations to give your cat-shaped cookies some purr-sonality!

Cat-ivity Fun!

Grab a pen, pencil, markers, or crayons and get ready for some fun cat-ivities!

Kitty Trivia

Think you know a lot about cats?
Test your feline knowledge with these trivia questions.

1 What's the average life expectancy for an *indoor* cat?
    A. 10 years
    B. 15 years
    C. 20 years

2 Do cats only purr when they are happy?

3 Who were the first people to have pet cats?
    A. Ancient Egyptians
    B. The Vikings
    C. Medieval Royalty

4 How does a cat keep itself clean?

5 What animal has better hearing, a dog or a cat?

6 Do cats have the same number of toes on each paw?

7 Does a cat spend more of its life awake or asleep?

8 Do cats sweat?

9 What kind of cat is almost always female?

10 Is having a pet cat good for your health?

Kitty Trivia Answers

1. **B. 15 years** (They usually live much longer than outdoor cats.)

2. **No** (Most of the time cats purr when they are content, but they are also known to purr when they are in pain or distress.)

3. **A. Ancient Egyptians** (Archeologists have discovered mummified cats in ancient Egyptian tombs.)

4. **With its tongue!**

5. **A cat**

6. **No** (They usually have five toes on their front paws and four toes on their back paws. Sometimes they even have extra toes!)

7. **Asleep** (On average, a cat will sleep for 16 hours every day!)

8. **Yes** (But only through their paws!)

9. **Tortoiseshell** (Tortoiseshell is a type of fur pattern, not a breed. Calicos belong to this group of colorful cats.)

10. **Yes** (Having a pet cat can lower your blood pressure!)

Scaredy Cat!

Give this kitty a Halloween costume!

Fancy Cat

Get Miss Kitty ready for the catwalk—
decorate her collar and give her some style!

Wordsearch

Find and circle the names of
different cat breeds hidden in the letters below.

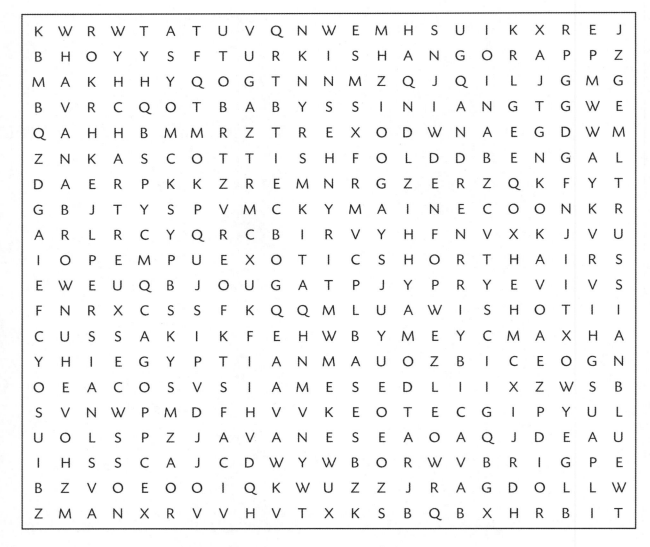

```
K  W  R  W  T  A  T  U  V  Q  N  W  E  M  H  S  U  I  K  X  R  E  J
B  H  O  Y  Y  S  F  T  U  R  K  I  S  H  A  N  G  O  R  A  P  P  Z
M  A  K  H  H  Y  Q  O  G  T  N  N  M  Z  Q  J  Q  I  L  J  G  M  G
B  V  R  C  Q  O  T  B  A  B  Y  S  S  I  N  I  A  N  G  T  G  W  E
Q  A  H  H  B  M  M  R  Z  T  R  E  X  O  D  W  N  A  E  G  D  W  M
Z  N  K  A  S  C  O  T  T  I  S  H  F  O  L  D  D  B  E  N  G  A  L
D  A  E  R  P  K  K  Z  R  E  M  N  R  G  Z  E  R  Z  Q  K  F  Y  T
G  B  J  T  Y  S  P  V  M  C  K  Y  M  A  I  N  E  C  O  O  N  K  R
A  R  L  R  C  Y  Q  R  C  B  I  R  V  Y  H  F  N  V  X  K  J  V  U
I  O  P  E  M  P  U  E  X  O  T  I  C  S  H  O  R  T  H  A  I  R  S
E  W  E  U  Q  B  J  O  U  G  A  T  P  J  Y  P  R  Y  E  V  I  V  S
F  N  R  X  C  S  S  F  K  Q  Q  M  L  U  A  W  I  S  H  O  T  I  I
C  U  S  S  A  K  I  K  F  E  H  W  B  Y  M  E  Y  C  M  A  X  H  A
Y  H  I  E  G  Y  P  T  I  A  N  M  A  U  O  Z  B  I  C  E  O  G  N
O  E  A  C  O  S  V  S  I  A  M  E  S  E  D  L  I  I  X  Z  W  S  B
S  V  N  W  P  M  D  F  H  V  V  K  E  O  T  E  C  G  I  P  Y  U  L
U  O  L  S  P  Z  J  A  V  A  N  E  S  E  A  O  A  Q  J  D  E  A  U
I  H  S  S  C  A  J  C  D  W  Y  W  B  O  R  W  V  B  R  I  G  P  E
B  Z  V  O  E  O  O  I  Q  K  W  U  Z  Z  J  R  A  G  D  O  L  L  W
Z  M  A  N  X  R  V  V  H  V  T  X  K  S  B  Q  B  X  H  R  B  I  T
```

Abyssinian	Persian	Manx	Korat
Chartreux	Scottish Fold	Ragdoll	Ocicat
Havana Brown	Bengal	Siamese	Russian Blue
Maine Coon	Egyptian Mau	Burmese	Turkish Angora
	Javanese	Exotic Shorthair	

Mouser Maze

Help kitty find her
way to the toy mouse!

Feline Fact Crossword

Write the answers to the questions in the corresponding squares. Hint: All the answers can be found in this book!

ACROSS

3. In Thailand, this breed is considered good luck.

6. With flat ears and big round eyes, this breed of cat looks like the feline version of an owl.

7. This breed was discovered 200 years ago and has had many names.

10. This is the largest breed of domesticated cat.

11. This breed's topcoat can be up to 5 inches long!

DOWN

1. Norwegian Forest cats were first brought to Norway by the _____.

2. This affectionate breed is often floppy when picked up.

4. This spotted cat is born with stripes.

5. This breed is similar to the cats of Ancient Egypt.

8. This breed has no tail!

9. Turkish Angoras will often have mismatched _____.

10. This is the Egyptian word for cat.

56

I Love Cats! Diary

Soft and furry, sweet and purry, what's not to love about cats? This diary is the purr-fect place for you to fawn over those fluffy, cuddly little bundles of joy and show your affinity for anything with whiskers!

Your Personal Feline Faves

Cutest cat breeds

_____

_____

Prettiest fur colors or patterns

_____

_____

Best names for a cat

_____

_____

Coolest famous cats

_____

_____

Favorite cat memory

_____

_____

_____

What I like best about cats

_____

_____

_____

Your Kitty's Favorite Things

Now write down your cat's faves.
(It's okay if your kitty is an imaginary one!)

Most appetizing foods

_____

_____

Yummiest treats

_____

_____

Best ways to pass the time

_____

_____

All-time fave toy

_____

_____

Fave place to be petted (or scratched)

_____

_____

Most comfortable sleeping spot

_____

_____

Favorite hangouts

_____

_____

_____

Paws-itively Adorable!

Use these pages to paste in the cutest kitty pics you can find—they can be of your sweet furball or of someone else's!

On the Hunt

Now put some of those old magazines
littered around your house to good use!
Clip out all the cute cats you can find and make
a collage of the images on these pages.

Artistic Mews

Ready to become a regular Pi-cat-so?
This is the place to leave your pawprints.
Decorate these pages with your kitty-cat doodle art!

Cat Tales

Tell your favorite cat story here—
such as how your fur-baby chose you, what
made you become crazy about cats, or the best
cat-venture you and a furry friend have shared!

Cats Me If You Can!

Admit it, your sweet baby can also be a furry terror.
What's the worst thing your
cat-astrophic kitty has ever done?

_____

_____

_____

_____

_____

_____

_____

_____

_____

_____

_____

All About

Name of Cat

_____

Birthday

_____

Adoption day

_____

_____

Adopted from breeder, friend or relative, shelter, or street?

_____

_____

_____

Fur length

_____

Fur color

Eye color

Weight

Nicknames

How/why did you choose your cat's name?

Meow-meries

Share more of your favorite cat memories here.

Picture Purr-fect!

Decorate these picture frames and then use tape or glue to attach your favorite kitty picture!

Kitty Dish

Decorate Kitty's food dish!

Sketch Pad

Now that you have practiced drawing all your favorite breeds step by step on scrap paper, you can fill the pages of this sketch pad with finished colored drawings. You can even decorate your scenes with the stickers in the back of this book!

Get a grown-up to help you cut out these fun accessories!

I'm busy!

But I'll cat-cha later!

Books are the cat's meow!

Reading is one purr-fect pastime!

Kitty crazy!

Do not Disturb!
(taking a cat nap)

I ♥ Cats!

Have an adult help you cut out these cute kitties so you can build your own scene!

Fold along the line to make the kitten stand up!

Decorate these postcards and mail them to a friend!

Place
Stamp
Here

Place
Stamp
Here